BLOODROOT

Bloodroot is so satisfying and compelling it's hard to believe it's Bill King's first book. These poems sing with confidence and music and wonder in a voice that is as nuanced as it is straightforward. Whether he's writing about the yard-long beans in his garden, or exploring a cave with his son, or waking up in the recovery room after yet another cancer surgery, King's poems are clear-eyed and open-hearted in a way that is both essential and healing.

—Doug Van Gundy, poet and director of the low-residency MFA Program in Writing, West Virginia Wesleyan College

Central Appalachia is one of the most biodiverse regions in the world. The land swarms with flora and fauna that bursts with life and death, both, with life as death, death as life. Not apathetic, never apathetic, never without booming celebration of color and flight, but with a certain knowing that death is both real and not real, that we creatures of the hill, we resurrect. *Bloodroot* knows what the land knows. Each of these exquisitely crafted, deeply ecological, humid poems accumulate into a *bildungsroman* for the grown. May it be taught alongside Ann Pancake's *Strange as This Weather Has Been* and Irene McKinney's *Have You Had Enough Darkness Yet?* May it be offered at every library, every hospital chapel, every seed store in the valleys. Bill King has given us an instant classic for the tradition.

—Rebecca Gayle Howell, author of *What Things Cost*

Beautiful, honest, generous, the poems in *Bloodroot* ask us to look closely at what we often call the dying world and instead see the thousand daily resurrections there. King carries hard-won wisdom on this subject, having experienced near deaths himself, then the grueling process of personal regeneration. I admire so much about this book, but this settles in me most deeply: *Bloodroot* gifts us sober hope and natural medicine for surviving, and loving, our world as it is now.

—Ann Pancake, author of *Strange as This Weather Has Been*

MERCER UNIVERSITY PRESS

Endowed by

TOM WATSON BROWN
and
THE WATSON-BROWN FOUNDATION, INC.

BLOODROOT

Poems

Bill King

MERCER UNIVERSITY PRESS
Macon, Georgia

MUP/ P682

© 2023 by Mercer University Press
Published by Mercer University Press
1501 Mercer University Drive
Macon, Georgia 31207
All rights reserved

27 26 25 24 23   5 4 3 2 1

Books published by Mercer University Press are printed on acid-free paper
that meets the requirements of the American National Standard for
Information Sciences—Permanence of Paper for Printed Library Materials.

Printed and bound in the United States.

This book is set in Adobe Garamond Pro.

Cover/jacket design by Burt&Burt.

ISBN   978-0-88146-910-3
Cataloging-in-Publication Data is available from the Library of Congress

for Beth, Walter, Elizabeth, and Josie

"I have seen the mountains, and here, they are wavering, and all the hills palpitate."

—Jeremiah 4:24

Acknowledgments

I gratefully acknowledge the editors of the following journals, books, and anthologies in whose pages the following poems first appeared.

About Place Journal: "Poem for My Night Nurse"

Appalachian Heritage: "Flight"; "Hawks at Dusk"

Appalachian Review: "Gathering Hickory Nuts Before the Examination"; "Post-Diagnosis"

Change Seven: "After the Argument;" "Promise Made in Total Darkness"

HeartWood: "Pre-Carnal Knowledge" (winner of the 2021 HeartWood Poetry Prize); "This Is the Way"

Kestrel: "Fifty Gardens In"

Mountains Piled upon Mountains: Appalachian Nature Writing in the Anthropocene (WVU Press): "Returning Me My Eyes"

Poecology: "Burning Inside the Glass Rim of the World"

Southern Poetry Anthology (Texas Review Press): "The Pond"

Still: The Journal: "Black Kite"; "Going Down the Hall on a Gurney"; "How to Destroy a Mountain"; "The Kite Master"; "The Wasp"

Stone River Sky: Anthology of Georgia Poetry (Negative Capability Press): "Winter Song"

Susurrus: A Literary Arts Magazine of the South: "A Song for the Doe-Thief"; "Living Wall"

The Letting Go (chapbook, Finishing Line Press): "Along the Staunton-Parkersburg Turnpike"; "At Thirteen"; "Beaver Pond"; "Burning Inside the Glass Rim of the World"; "Crossing the Eastern Continental Divide at Sundown"; "Even the Wild Iris"; "Flight" (as

"The Letting Go"); "First Things"; "Going Down the Hall on a Gurney"; "Hawks at Dusk"; "How to Destroy a Mountain"; "Returning Me My Eyes"; "The Least of These"; "The Pond"; "This Is the Way"; "This World Should Be Enough"; "To the Boy Whose Blood I Shed"; "When Love Returns"; "Winter Song"

I am grateful for Gordon Johnston and Doug Van Gundy, whose keen eyes and ears made these poems better. These poems could not exist without the abiding support and faith of my wife Beth, my daughter Elizabeth and her wife, Josie, and my son, Walter. The spoken and written words of Maggie Anderson, Marc Harshman, and Ann Pancake helped me push on. Finally, a special thanks goes to Katherine Osborne and Rob Phillips of Davis & Elkins College, who made a space for this book to be completed.

CONTENTS

1. GROWN BOY

2. BLACK KITE

3. THIS WORLD SHOULD BE ENOUGH

4. TO HAVE AND TO HOLD

5. FIFTY GARDENS IN

1.

GROWN BOY

The Other Side of the Road

The day the hit dog bit me
it was the summer of 1977,
blazing hot in southwest Virginia
along the two-mile stretch
between my house
and Rierson's grocery.

I'd come down the mountain
on the little trail beneath
the poplars and pines
to the creek, hopped over,
and then rowed through
the tall grass to the road,
where I kept to the little strip
of gravel between the tar
and the ditch.

I saw the dog, a beagle mix
wide-eyed and stunned,
as soon as I hit the main road
where the cars and timber trucks
whipped past so fast they'd
take your hat off. He picked
his head up upon my approach
and I squatted down—

Oh you poor boy—my hand outstretched,
and that's when he lunged,
snarled, and snapped in one
motion so quick it was like
the first time I'd been bit
by the electric fence in

the cow meadow over the hill
from school.

He struggled up and into the weeds
as I fell back. I left him to die—
I am sure of it. I never told anyone.
I just drank my Coke, ate my crackers,
and played a dollar's worth of pinball
before walking home
on the other side
of the road.

How Not to Be Seen

Sometimes, when the screen door slammed behind,
a ruffed grouse would explode through the pines.
Don't slam the damned door, father would bellow.
Slow the hell down! So I learned to walk toe to heel

out of the house. Mostly, I'd head to the creek,
fish for chubs or flip rocks for crawdads. If you still,
and form a shadow with your hand, silt will pass
and one come clear, casting about two antennae

as if in search of a signal. People require more stealth.
Smear your face and chest with mud. If you hear
a car downshift into the curve by the dump, freeze
like a rabbit and squat. Watch it flash through

sassafras on the far bank and look away if the face
in the window turns toward the bright green bog
between you and the road. When he passes
the orange lilies and slows, you can stand,

slide a pinch of bread onto the hook until the point
just pricks through the dough. This is how not to be
seen—a cloaked hook, an empty claw beneath a stone
chamber, waiting for the moon.

Carp

By the time we grew tall enough to see out
the window, into paradise—
we were encouraged to think of ourselves

as ghosts, exiles called to table each evening
to take on our bodies and bow our heads
dear lord, for these and all our blessings,

which, as far as we were concerned,
existed beyond the door and down
the hill to the creek along the one-lane,

or zagging skyward up the mountain,
until we could speed into town to fish
the big water with white bread

and a bobber. Once, it was a carp
a man framing apartments came down
to see. *Carp,* he said, as I looked up,

then held my rod
while I unhooked
and walked him back to water.

Brother-Fort

Here comes the mailman—I knew
the sound of the jeep and time of day—
downshifting into the curve above the creek
where generations dumped old tires,

a Frigidaire, and a thousand broken jars,
bits of blue we spit-cleaned and held
up to the sun cutting through the pines.
We wedged them in the bark

of sentry trees standing guard
at the entrance to our lean-to:
deadfall woven with evergreen
for walls and a roof, until it rained,

and back at the dump, we discovered
the *coup de grâce*—discarded carpet
that once lugged over stepping stones
and unrolled, blotted out the sky.

This was below the house on the ridge,
between the trillium and bloodroot,
whose petals fall just as soon
as the flower begins to bloom.

Burning Inside the Glass Rim of the World

Through honey stripes of August light long in the pines,
Sumter's dogs fly for two boys topping out their ten speeds
along a ridgeline striped gray with gravel. They pump hard,
until a man from some porch beyond the grove bellows
and the thin-legged hounds, as if chained to his word, pull up
short, point noses high, and stand plumbing what's left of our dust.

We shoot past them as if steering bright new kayaks into the narrow
gorge below—red beating blue around the bend and down
the chute—and that is when I see big brother rise out of his seat,
and with green eyes singing shout something over his shoulder
I cannot possibly catch: wind rushing like water in ear, legs and lungs
aflame and burning everything in our wake—the pines and the cows

and the corn leaves, their brown tongues rasping ruin as we pass,
as we take the long, slow curve into that narrow valley for good.
We stand high on our pedals then, bodies abuzz with speed and heat
and light, before gliding by the same little metal row of neighbors,
nailed to the same swaybacked plank, their moon-straight flags
all fallen now, their thin prim lips slammed shut for the day.

Grown Boy Dreams of Water

I'm carrying a bucket down the mountain
again, looking for the creek's moon-glint

because my mother's rock garden is dry,
but the closer I get, the more the water

curves away. I go off-trail, trying to correct,
but arm-thick laurel weaves green hells,

closing overhead, and as their pink buds swell,
I'm climbing—towards a keyhole that opens

into a bald of boulders. Here, above tree-line,
the sky is a kerosene globe trimmed low

enough for stars, which I see from the bottom
of my father's johnboat—hauled from South

Carolina to central Appalachia and beached
on the edge of a field. Sometimes, I'd unlean

it from its pine, tug it through tall grass, and stare
into a deep blue ocean. For a time, I fit between

the bench seats prone—a tiny bone in the boat's
deep ear, intent on the sound of water.

The Pond

Because two horses
lifted their heads beneath
an apple tree at the top of the hill
and snorted

I waded across the creek
slipped beneath the barbed wire
that stitched the hem
of old man Warner's field

and rowed my arms
through late summer grass
before stepping out of the field
and into the rut
the horses had made
to gorge on sweet green apples
spotted with mold

From beneath this tree
I first saw old man Warner's pond
pushing clouds along the earth
and that is when I first saw everything
that was between here and there

the smell of clover and carrion
the snap of grasshopper wings
the sudden cross of a red-tail blown sideways
and circling
watching everything below
even the bullfrogs flopping and turtles sliding
into dark water

I walked full 'round twice
not knowing what I had found
nor that this was the first of a thousand future leavings
of which I still can never tell anyone
where or why I am going

To the Boy Whose Blood I Shed

Naked boy from across the holler
up Whitehall and down dirt road
to the meadow, you were popping
beavertails with cupped hands
so loudly in the fishing hole below
I could hear your joy through the trees
from where I lay behind the house
staring out of a ditch
into leaves and sky.

I was still sore from picking
bees off our bloodhound Dan,
whose bewildered howl
I could hear from a mile away—
as the bus came 'round
the curve before the final stretch,
as we braked into the hairpin
that crossed the creek
and labored up the mountain.

When those double doors flopped
open I dropped my books and ran—
the sky and the grass and the trees
fleery with tears—
to where I'd clipped him on the run
between the pines I'd picked
for its sun and shade,
for its soft bed of needles,
and for its view of the woods
that as a pup he'd smudged
every window in the house
to see.

I have to tell you:
when I heard your naked joy in the creek
where I had swum and, descending the trail
that runs from the house to the hole,
picked up that perfectly weighted rock—
when I let it fly—
Dan was still fresh in the ditch I'd dug
in the back corner where the garden goes
to blackberry in the sun.

How was I to know
about the nest beneath the stump?
How was I to know about self-hatred
and regret?

Boy from across the
holler and up Whitehall road,
for all I know you're
resting in the meadow now. But I'm
sorry, anyway, for you
and all of us—
whose human hearts
have many chambers
that hold old pains deep,
until you scratch one up.

Listening to In-a-Gadda-Da-Vida with Steve

The summer of 1980, before my first shift
at Western Steer carving rot from potatoes
not fast enough or well, all I wanted was
a turntable to play 45s. Once I made some
money and could make it into town, I would
fly like an eagle, through the revolution,
but usually, I just rode my bike to Steve's,
who the girls all loved—his crashing wave of beach
blonde hair blazing brighter in the mountains—
though now I know that he was gay, and just
so lonesome he could cry.

       We listened to In-a-Gadda-Da-Vida
while his mother, shut up across the hall, just kept
sitting on a dock of the bay smoking dope with Otis
Redding, wasting time. I never saw her, and Steve
never said anything, just that she wasn't coming out
because she needed that song to play. So I kept
riding down the hill to find a singer that knew
our own particular brand of blues: how to be true
to the rich girls in the valley neither of us,
for our different and pointless reasons,
would ever be able to love.

Symphony in G Minor

At 13, I stop walking to church,
my father having long left it back
in South Carolina, leaving
my mother to point the way.

When we move onto the mountain,
I choose the room facing the holler's
far ridge. Gray poplar and white pine
march down one side and up the other

and at the desk before the open window
I begin to type poems as long as the sound
of the creek below, where fins wimpling
gravel had yet to write their name—

Salvelinus fontinalis, little salmon of the springs—
in the Ferlinghetti of my mind. On a visit south,
my uncle asks what sport I'll play. When I don't
answer, he sizes me up, says, *cross-country rewards*

the stubborn, so rather than trading blows
with boys learning the language of bullies,
I run deer trails all summer that wrap around
the mountain's sides like arteries do the heart.

That fall, with Mozart's Symphony in G blasting out
my father's window—over the tidy meadow I'd cleared
and mowed—I argue in favor of brush piles full of birds
until he douses them with gas and hands me the match.

Why I Can Stand Here Now Telling You This Story

beginning with a line from Mark Jarman

When things began to happen and I knew it,
I was thirteen, going on fourteen, hanging
out with my adopted friend Ben, who, though

welcomed by those foreign to him, stole change
from his father's sock drawer (*because he's* not *my
father*, he said) before breaking into the country

store at the bottom of Bent Mountain. At Rierson's,
farmers filled up trucks and teenagers smelling
of chicken shit drank soda and played pinball

after a shift packing eggs. He went to jail for that,
and though not as smart as him, I was the one who
drove down the mountain to college. Once, free

after school until our parents came home, Ben
showed me how to ping hubcaps from the ridge
below my house, over-pumping the Remington

and sighting over the creek and through the pines
at the occasional car weaving its way along
the narrow road, sinuous as a black snake

sunning in the grass. I took my shot at a green
station wagon moving slow as a hearse
but heard nothing, until a policeman's tires

churned gravel in the drive an hour later.
He stepped out of a blue-gray cloud
to find me whittling on the porch. *No sir,*

I said, hardly glancing up from my chunk
of wood. *We were throwing rocks over the creek.*
That was a walking stick in my hand. I had not

yet even asked a girl to dance, but there I sat
telling stories like I was born to it and couldn't stop.
May I be struck dead where I stand, I said

to my father, later, looking square into his smalt-
colored eyes. And because I wasn't, by him
or God—I turned my back and walked.

2.

Black Kite

Songbirds, Midwinter

I live dead center in the Tygart River
Valley, which is expanding, now, with light.
On frog-pond ice, a chickadee tips
his cap each time he dips at the base of a leaf
that's billowed just enough, night-long,
to fashion a crack of water.
I did not always feel this way—or soon
enough—but when the mountains
begin to pink, I am a half-buried wick
that won't stay lit for long. Still,
everything glows. It winks.
In the rose, a sparrow whistles a tune
it took a full season for me to heed—
there's a time to be silent and a time to speak.
When I wipe my eyes, they've gone.

Before Words

Before sitting down to write, I cut bloody william, white aster,
and primrose from the strip between the yard and the alley—
bring them in and arrange for show. Why? I don't know.

A marriage of *mystery and manners*, I suspect: a reconstruction,
like this shed, 6 x 7 x 6, made of houses knocked and razed.
Bent tin, boards with bad ends—once squared and ripped—

are good for resurrection. This morning, through uncaulked
cracks, the howl of wind and fire trucks almost rhyme. Branches
bend and clack. Hail like rock salt pelts the roof—all rolls

and rolls like a runaway train into this narrow valley where
I wasn't born but have always lived, with a river running through.
When I was four, my mother visited a friend between the James

and the tracks. It was the longest ride of my life.
But there was a boy named Jimmy with a penny and a dime.
We put them down, then scrambled as the engine blared.

When time came to go and she packed me for home, I didn't
have words for the shine in her eyes. Just a piece of coal
and the silver and gold the wheels had left behind.

Waking up in Recovery

A stream of light like noonday sun through the canopy
burns my eyes, which close again—then seep, but do not run.

Further down, a frozen grade. Fingertips, like bike tires
over tracks, bump sternum to pelvis, then take a right.

Staples, someone says—a word I begin to circle like a crow
does a snake in the road.

Your Time and Mine

after David Huddle

What can I say worth your time and mine?
sans emoticon, sans meme, mellifluous and wise?
Well, if art is *a strange object...that breaks*
your heart, just look around and weep:
sparrows dart then land in the pothole
across the street. Shudder in cool water—
heat shimmering in the lot behind. Last night's
rain abides. It perks what's left of the garden,
lifts the wings of swallowtails—tickseed
to coneflower to cosmos—and speeds
the beat of hummers working the colors
of sunrise: pink cleome, scarlet runner,
jewelweed hanging by a thread. It's been
a good run. No flash in the pan. Open
the windows and doors. Preserve what you can.

Hosanna at Guy and Elm

*a response to the popular location
encoding system What3Words*

Here on the edge of Guy Street,
in a former treehouse more win-
dow than wall, lowered one rep-

urposed board at a time and rep-
ieced beneath a buckeye, a map-
le, and a willow, within earshot

of a 200-gallon-give-or-take-go-
ldfish pond, down from 21, 12
years ago to 7, one more white

than gold,12 water spiders, one
green frog and a periodical drag-
onfly, three dogs barking, two in

the alley with joy and one more
urgently on a leash behind me in
the street, one sparrow in the je-

welweed framed by the door, now
joining the ones, well two, no thr-
ee pulling leaves from the top-mo-

st beans, its pie plates clashing in-
effectively, followed, now, by the
tinny jingle of the stray's new be-

ll, foretelling what I cannot see, s-
he slipping beneath the fence tow-
ard her hiding spot in the hosta—

I can't fathom why we need to *div-
ide the world into a grid of 57 trillion
3x3 meter squares, each of which has a*

three-word address, and yet, *hotspots.
ambient.gloriously* describes the clou-
ds building directly above the four-

piece tin roof of this 11-stanza, 31-li-
ne, 946-character tower of gratitude
(not counting the spaces in between).

June Bug

Devotee of the noonday sun,
you travel up and out of the dark earth,
summit the tallest weed,
and seemingly stunned by your mere existence,
split a slick green shield,
revealing a set of clear, veined wings
thin as microfilm.

High above my head,
you empty your emerald energy into
an inscrutable spin, looping like a tiny balloon
let loose at a party before
the end—

a reckless descent
one could only hope but follow,
bouncing off the elephant ears of sunflowers,
through the purple trunks of okra,
before crashing downside up
beneath a tangle of tomato vines
ablaze with yellow stars.

A Song for the Doe-Thief

In the pre-dawn fog before the log trucks' rumble
and old folks (like me) perk their morning coffee,
the big doe descends (again) to graze on lilies

unfolded—yellows, golds, and pastel pinks (I'm told)
hauled all the way from my sister-in-law's,
four states south in Georgia. Three years in a row.

You'd think I'd learn. Two-toeing concrete, asphalt,
ghosting six-foot fences, yard to yard to yard,
until she finds (again) that Shangri-La—

that nirvana of unburst suns in the devil's strip
between sidewalk and the road. Who can blame her?
One could do worse, I think, than map the world

with nose and eye and tongue. Which is why her theft
of my in-law's gift has not been cursed but sung.

Living Wall

Out the seeds' first leaves—twin hearts
that point in opposite directions—tri-fingered
vines climb slash pole and mason string
to make a living wall: a summer screen
between my neighbor and me, filtering
laughter and deepening silence, except when
the robin sings. He'll sit above the property
line reminding us how to breathe. To this
great height the beans aspire. Yard longs, this year.
Skinny and sweet, with dark green and glossy leaves.
By late July, we'll no longer wave. We'll angle
our heads like cats in the wild to find a line of sight.
They look ready to me, I'll say, when at last we meet.
Take what you need. I've more than I can eat.

Fireflies Rise at the Garden Party

Cicadas and goldenrod herald an end
to genteel gin and tonic—berries soon gone
to the birds or, best, my deep freeze
for me to mix in with the ice and lime
I'd serve to Muhammed Ali, if I could,
and Mahatma Gandhi—and shoot—
let's throw in MLK, a quorum of the greats
who imagined a place where tear gas,
firehoses, and unleashed dogs
no longer rule the day.

I'd stand aside, invisible as a waiter
beneath the stippled light of maple,
looking out beyond their heads—their skin
gilded now by the last rays of sun—into the garden,
and know how one man or woman's lilting voice
can lift me up to where we're all headed
like ten thousand strong
catching fire
and rising.

At Thirteen

Above Guy Street winds push the birthday
plane, a silver P-51, into a stall: a look
of dread flashes across the boy-pilot's face
as if he, too, even with feet square on ground,

is falling. He guns the prop and banks
hard but still whirs into the uppermost
branches of a leafless maple, and because I
know the feeling that causes that look, say,

"Hang tight," and go for the garage where
every manner of broken thing awaits its
resurrection. Even with extension rod and
ladder I fall short, until I remember the

buckeye branch leaning against the house
and try again—standing on tiptoe two rungs
from the top and half way up the tree—to lift
the plane up and out. I'm closer this time

but for that feel the futility all the more,
until with neck cramping and eyes watering,
see first one and then another balloon
from some other party in some other corner

of the county hit the jet stream. They make me
want to say something—about the balloons,
the wind that may knock the plane loose in the night,
anything that could make this seem less unfair—

but, instead, I step one last rung higher
and make one last inadvisable stab
that jars the plane loose. Cartwheeling free—
he guns it again, and soars back into blue.

Going Down the Hall on a Gurney

Beneath a silver sky
men on mowers sheer
the wild green tongues
of a meadow. But that
must have been yesterday
because now half a dozen boys,
each as straight and tall as a little *i*
bend in the middle towards home,
singing *Hey batter batter,*
listen to my chatter, batter batter—
Suh-wing!—an incantation cracked
open by wood on ball rising
so high it is a tiny comet skirting
the sun. It is streaking towards
a horse that always grazes
in the pasture beyond, and now
the leftfielder launches; he hangs
suspended—I can see him clearly,
as if I were lying
in the grass beneath:
the glove hand, open wide
for something he can
never snare; the red cap,
name and number scrawled
black under the brim;
the red t-shirt, plump white *P*
over the heart; and blue
bell bottoms, yellow paisley
patches on each knee,
stretched tight and let out
twice for legs that trail
like a great heron

taking flight. Such awkward
beauty, I think—trying to make
out the face—
until the slightly parted lips
of a woman droop
into view; they lean
like a heavy bloom over
a still spring pool.
Can you tell me your name?
they say, *And can you tell me
your date of birth? Yes,*
I say, to the white blunt petals
of bloodroot that flutter
as she breathes. *I was born
in May,* I say to the purple
woods behind them.
I was born in May.

Post-Diagnosis

When I moved to this town, there was a man who shuffled up
and down the drag—slow as a tugboat pulling an invisible load.
His head slumped but he kept his blue twill work shirt ironed

and matching pants cinched tight. Once, when I passed him
on the street and nodded, he stopped, looked me in the eyes,
and made the sound of a kid-size motor bike that goes round

and round. Now, I understand that no one really understands.
It's why, at the end of the block, rather than leaning into the turn
as I have for years, I keep going, into a field hemmed and

humming with rose. Once cleared for cows that sunk fetlock deep
in this creek, now it's blackberry and wingstem. Here and there
a pokeweed—blood red and heavy with fruit. You have to find

a deer trail through—a chest-high crease that catches at clothing,
then closes behind as you go. Today is hot and humid. Cicada,
like a pressure canner thrumming on the stove, and over that,

the cry of two sharp-shins, then crows. Like them, I want to tell
you what I feel. I want words to see me through. In the cool
of the wood, a young doe watches. She's waiting for me to move.

Poem for My Night Nurse

Tied down by tubes in my nose, neck, and arms,
I watch the second hand on the wall clock spin
like a slow-motion roulette wheel; when the minute
hand hits my number, I press the pain button.
I want to stand as soon as possible but know I can't,
that like Gulliver, I'm washed up on a strange island.
I'm Frankenstein's creature, one hand outstretched,
muttering inarticulate sounds.

But unlike his master, who sparked life, then fled,
my night nurse abides. When I croak like a raven,
she wets my lips and asks if, in the morning, I want
a sponge bath. I do. *First the bath and then I'll stand,*
I think again and again, until she comes in, asks
if the water is warm enough, and starts to work her way
down my body.

Yes, I say, and *thank you*, which is not enough
in this shockingly foreign country where everyone's pain
is equal and you're always at the front of the line.

Sunday Circuit

Chemo courses through like a deep river under ice.
Looking out the frost-flecked window, no gibbous moon
as I had thought. But a dusting covers everything;
and looking down to tongue and groove—the white
stamps of sparrow prints when wings
erased the snow.

      It's hard to take, some days, this Sunday
circuit down the block and up. But, sometimes,
above town, the houses seem to float; I'm
the youngest again, bumping like a balloon
from under my brother's bunk, across
the room and out.

      So I open the door, and eyes water—blazing
every surface. Clearing vision with the heels of my hands,
the world takes shape as if for the first time—as I topple
rime-glazed grass, turn down-alley, and climb
above the broad arms of oaks to the tall green
masts of pine.

      By now, blood pounds in my ears; I bend
at the knees, see brain-stars swimming in the leaves.
Gripping thighs, I peer forward—a little herd of deer
across the holler's staring back. No huff, no wag.
No warning flags. Just this tight rope gaze
I cross.

Gathering Hickory Nuts before the Examination

This time of year, the morning fog—cloaking rain
or sun—makes no promises. But come what may,
there's always work to be done: dead-head the marigolds,
survey the garden, removing what no longer fruits.

Instead, you rattle the mower into position and pull
the cord for the last cut of the season. Soon, the dull
blades are knocking off the dark brown husks of hickory
nuts that have dropped, then rolled, from the tree—

some, all the way to the road. The rest—spit out
as hard white shells you'll gather to crack, but not
before dumping in water to tell the good from the bad,
keeping the ones that sink. After lunch, sit on the crinkly

white paper of the examination table until the doctor
comes in, asks you to lie back, then begins to press
his fingertips beneath your ribcage (*yes*, you say, *but
it's always tender where they took it away*) to just above

your pelvis (*and* there, *where it came back*). Don't ask,
How long? You get what you get. Knock the hulls off
a hundred lives and most will float like ghosts; they're
shriveled and hollow before they even hit the ground.

The Wasp

Like green willows cut back, then cut
again, the surgeon's scalpel removes each
season's stubborn new growth, stunted
by poisonous drip. I zombie to work

and back, yet live, and in living, love
and grieve all those who came before,
who risked and lost—pounds of flesh
and good-time friends, and that one

last hope, before the end. I can't call it
a win—what they've given. Time.
To scrutinize eternity—as carefully
as this wasp perched on the rounded

hill of my eraser. Forced out the vent
by the first furnace blast of the year,
she makes one tiny-footed, antennae-
twitching rotation, before flying

toward the arched forest of golden
fern just outside the window.
Trapped, she bumps from glass
to glass, seeking late autumn light.

Though frost soon rimes the grass,
and I've little energy to muster,
I offer the sugared lip of my coffee
cup and walk her out the door.

In the Waiting Room

While we sit masked in the waiting room, choking down contrast,
the slab on the wall sells perpetual youth with the morning news—
porous borders, rockets from Gaza, bumper to bumper on 376.
Status quo. Though, each of knows, change is on the way.

I'm from West Virginia, I say to the nurse who draws my blood, *between
Snowshoe and Canaan. Yes, it's pretty there,* and think things you do not share:
how, at this hour, my garden is bathed in late May light and the song
sparrow trills atop the Old Man's Beard, trembling, now, with lace.

Back to my chair to wait. Everyone still tuned to the morning news.
So I close my eyes in time to see the bird fly over the lawn into the maple
where he takes it up again, an aubade so insistent mind and body
disarray—

William K? William K? Then I'm one body length behind Robert P,
walking to Radiology, where I'll fiddle with a gown, lay down,
and be scanned—collar bone to pelvis by a machine that swallows me
then intones, *Hold your breath,*

which I do and have been doing going on eight years now, though not
metaphorically, having taken my cue from the pawpaw I planted by the road.
It tastes like banana and mango but doesn't keep, so you can't buy it
in the store. I don't think, anymore,

about how long it takes to fruit. Just that, burned by frost, the little tree
re-leafs. It'll do it again and again. Which is to say, all this cutting
and blasting has granted so much more time—when the surgeon comes
to tell me the news, I close my eyes and fly.

Black Kite

Rain drummed, then tapped all night, before changing to snow.
Around dawn, limbs popped like gunshots and, three days later,
I was thirty feet up a curly willow, looking down on houses

gutter to gutter. Salt-melt in the alley. Across the street,
two mechanics twisting stubs into a sand-filled coffee can and,
fingers numbing, I had no inkling of the body-doubling pain

that would force me down the ladder, into the emergency room—
to a doc-in-the-box because it had to be cheaper, then back
to the emergency room because, by then, I could hardly stand.

Now that I've survived five years—albeit cut back by three surgeries
and two bouts of chemo, folks look at me like I ought to know something.
Do you pray? they ask. *We prayed for you every day.* Well, I say,

I go for short hikes or, sometimes, just sit in the kitchen glassing birds.
This satisfies the majority. Others nod, though, wanting more. So, once,
I told this one: last week a friend took me to the state park. Blackwater.

You know. To the cliff overlook. We walk past the slot binoculars
and onto a rock slab jutting like a ship's prow above the canyon.
Downriver, dark water like a black thread stitched through green.

I squat, edge toward the rock's lip, then swing my legs into the void.
What happened? they ask. Arms prickling, I see, again, the vulture rising
updraft like a kite. *Nothing*, I say. *You should try it.*

3.

This World Should Be Enough

Winter Song

after W. S. Merwin

I miss the spring peeper
who crawled out
the rain fed pond
all summer
until each one
green and wood frogs too
buried themselves in mud
beneath ice or snow

and I miss the first big rain
that made little throats trill
from bent stems
of elderberry and curly willow
from green leaves of young maple
that shade the street
behind the grocer
that faces state route 33
and the rest of the world

all of this has gone now
unfleshed except for sky
scarred with jet trails
going anywhere but here

lover of evening rain
lover of last light
lover of small still water
that gazes at leaves
all summer

come back

First Things

In my yard, white blooms first:
snowdrop, pussy willow, service berry.
Petals come of nothing, it seems.
Purple, the color of memory,
follows—hyacinth, crocus,
and sweet william

along the stream, where little
brook trout nose the current—
their thin sleek bodies
the color of sunrise,
pebbled orange,
turning blue.

Even the Wild Iris

The little sparrows in the box
chatter *want, want*
and are given.

They look out,
one at a time,
and the world is green

below, and above,
through the maple—
a winking blue.

They do not know,
yet, that there is a price
for flight.

How snow and ice cover all,
even the wild iris
with its slender

blue tongue,
first to rejoice
in spring.

Along the Staunton-Parkersburg Turnpike

The jonquil, buried forever
it must have seemed, in darkness,
now rise like small spears
through moss and maple leaf.
Even after the dinner bell
and shouts of children dimmed,
even as the old house fell
and its good boards were
trucked away,
the outline of little suns
continued to mark where the front
door opened like a mouth
to the mountains draped
in early morning fog.
Come late summer,
where corn once marched
toward the deep green wood,
the joepye and ironweed
will reign as tall as farm boys
waving as they go off to war—
not knowing, yet,
that they're not coming back.

The Least of These

I've parked in the turnout, at the head of a trail
to a favorite stream where, come spring,
little brookies leave the bed, shed stripes for spots—
and there, like toppled statues, lie two dumped deer,
their heart-shaped hooves pointing directly at me.
They're pre-bloat fresh and beautiful, save for a pair
of long wounds like open-cut mines along the ridge
of the spine where their backstraps used to be.
The best is always stripped, the rest left to lie.
Coyote, crow, and maggot will surely take the rest,
but, I think, as I pull the least one down the bank:
Who gives us the right to take so little from a kill?
Is there anybody home in that house on the hill?

History of Extraction Run Backwards

A roar of machines like revved dirt bikes at a starting
line raises an ocean of second growth trees, shuddering,
into silence, shrinks a shelf cloud west, untrapping the sun
and bluing the sky into orange, garnet, violet, and star star
star, then milky way, meteor, and firefly, dropping slow
into the blinking grass. The last notes of birds go silent
in the canopy and soon thin brown trails blazing gaps
between mountains piled upon mountains close,
muffling the shouts of men—

        until each one of those mountains slips into a shallow
sea swallowing tree fern and horsetail smashed black and flat
for miles. This was long before the first mammal unbent its back,
before tools, before the axe and saw and the clever ravenous teeth
of draglines hauled over earth unburdened by 5.5 million pounds
of ammonium nitrate and fuel oil each day, six days a week,
finally unmoored the wrecked green heart of Appalachia
and sent her downriver into the open mouth
of America.

The River Drivers, Braxton County, West Virginia, 1897

Afloat ten thousand board feet of pine,
the river driver stills himself. Perhaps
a fog has lifted and, though past noon,
the subject instructed to remove his broad-

brimmed hat to better capture his ghostly,
mustachioed face. Before and behind, a sea
of virgin trees limbed and cut and jammed—
landed after the first big flood. Stock straight

above the dark bullseye of the thickest one,
does he feel the tree's boom and shudder
through his cleats? And what of the other two
men against the far bank's smattering of unfelled

lumber? One seems the trunk of a living tree
placed under arrest—his leafless arms upstretched.
The other, downriver, stands on logs so washed
out and bright he is a condemned man hung

ropelessly—or a small black angel, levitating.
It's not that I wouldn't do as they have done.
I just want to start at the beginning, shameless
and free, under the first day's dark canopy.

A Century After the Battle of Blair Mountain

Seeking Cincinnati, having rolled out of the mountains—
its miles of track littered with coal coked hard and gray
in Bretz and Barrakville, Richard and Rachel, bound
for blast towns—Wheeling, Weirton—steeling for war.

Having crossed the muddy Ohio, land of cow and lamb,
and hit route 9, its dank fields darkening on the periphery—
a not dog, not fox, but coyote looks, then leaps long nose
first out the sparkling glass at the edge of the road,

just a flash, then safely out of vision for good. Until, next
morning, outside the Millennium Hotel. I'm about to walk
past a young man with a beard streaked red and gray—
still rolling along, programmed for the day—but he looks

like the striking miner captured in *The Saturday Evening Post*
years ago. Instead of a long rifle, though, he holds a word
in his hands: *Homeless*. Returning his gaze, I see what remains
a century after the last shot: the face of his father and of

his father's father, who emerged from the ground—
again and again—to launch a thousand ships. Flaring
with shame to smelt the heart, I say *Good morning, brother*,
fishing pockets for the least of what any of us should muster.

How to Destroy a Mountain

NOTE: Text taken from Master Teacher Mary McMurtry's "Cookie Monster's Delight: Grades 3-5" (published online by the Educational Broadcasting Corporation and the National Training Institute, 2006) and Carol Warren's "This Land Will Never Be for Sale," an interview with Larry Gibson, (published in the Ohio Valley Environmental Coalition's *Like Walking onto another Planet*, 2006, a collection of oral history interviews about mountaintop removal/valley fill activities in Appalachia) create this narrative in two voices.

1. First give each student a hard and a soft chocolate chip cookie
   on a napkin.
   > *When I was a kid, our place was like a wonderland.*
   > *People used to make fun of me*
   > *and say I was my father's retarded son.*
   > *They'd call me that, you know?*
   > *One of the things they couldn't understand*
   > *was that I was always able to get close to the wild animals.*
   > *I'd go out in the woods*
   > *and come home with a bobcat or a squirrel or a coon.*

2. Tell student that the cookies represent West Virginia's coal
   deposits.
   > *We never had toys.*
   > *The only toys we had was in the Spiegel catalog*
   > *when we went to the bathroom.*
   > *But it was a wonderland, you know?*
   > *You could walk through the forest. You could hear*
   > *the animals. The woods like to talk to you. You could feel*
   > *a part of Mother Nature. In other words, everywhere*
   > *you looked there was life. Now you put me on the same*
   > *ground where I walked, and the only thing you can feel*
   > *is the vibration of dynamite*
   > *or heavy machinery.*
   > *No life, just dust.*

3. Instruct student to count how many visible chunks of coal
   are in their state (cookie).

> *That Massey fellow was on TV the other day*
> *—he's the one I met with back in '92.*
> *And he told me my land was worth a million*
> *dollars an acre to the coal company then.*
> *Now recently they tell me that my land*
> *is now— since George Bush got into office—*
> *worth $450 million dollars. And they told me six*
> *months ago that by the time he gets out of office*
> *it will be escalated up to $650 million.*

4. Record data on chalkboard.

> *And he turns around and offers $140,000 for it.*

   Have students also record their own in the journals.

> *You know, it was like we didn't know*
> *the difference. Even if we wanted to sell,*
> *he was talking to us like they were really gonna*
> *do us a favor. "We're gonna help y'all out,*
> *make a generous offer to you."*
> *And he'd just told me*
> *it was worth over a million dollars.*

5. Have each student predict how many coal deposits they think
   are in their cookie.

> *I really didn't start having violence until I surveyed*
> *my own land. The land has been in the family for over*
> *220 years and had never been surveyed by anybody*
> *in the family except me. So when I did survey the land,*
> *I found that it had always been surveyed in behalf*
> *of the oil company, a utility company, a coal company*
> *but never in behalf of the people.*
> *I started forcing them back on the boundaries*
> *where they was supposed to be*
> *and that's when the violence started.*

   Have each student record predictions in journals.

They shot my dog,
they burned my cabin,
they set my pickup in the creek.
I never know when the trouble's coming for me.

6. Give each student a toothpick to mine their deposits.
    Hear that quiet?
Have them just mine ONE cookie first.
    You know they're about to set off a shot
    when they shut down the machines.
Make a pile of chocolate chips and one pile of the cookie crumbs.
    I used to look up at the mountains.

7. Count coal deposits and record and compare with estimate.
    But now I look down on them.

8. Before they mine the last cookie give them instructions that
   this time they are going to try to do the least amount of damage
   to the land as possible.
    We lost about 80, well,
    close to a hundred headstones in the family cemetery,
    because every time the coal company would blast,
    they'd blast debris over into the cemetery.
    It would bust some of the headstones,
    turn some of 'em over.
Instruct students to work carefully and offer a prize for the land
that is the least damaged.
    Then they'd send a crew of men over to clean them up.
    And then the old sandstone headstones that had carving
    on them, we caught them actually throwing them away,
    destroying them as well. And the simple reason behind that
    was to prove that we didn't have as many graves
    there on the ground as we had.
    And so, if they could reclaim some of the gravesites—well,
    the mountain had 39 seams of coal.
    There's a lot of wealth underneath there.

9. Ask which was more difficult to mine, the first or second cookie?
> *He was talking to us like they were really gonna do us a favor.*
> *When he said that, I said, "The land'll never be for sale.*
> *You can have my right arm, but you'll never get the land."*

The hard or soft cookie?
> *So he said, "Well, you know, you're the island*
> *and we are the ocean. You set in the middle of 187,000 acres*
> *of coal company land. You're the only thing we don't own*
> *between here and the Virginia border. I don't give a damn*
> *about nobody or nothing up in that holler.*
> *I only care about coal.*
> *You're gonna be one little green island up there."*

Who is going to fix the land after the mining of their cookie
is done?
> *I don't know what the answer is as far as what's happening.*
> *Destroying all the environment—all the streams.*
> *When I was a kid, down at the bottom of the mountain,*
> *I could get crawdads, pick them up out of the water*
> *with my toes.*
> *Now nothing lives in the water. Nothing lives on the land.*
> *What they've done is irreversible. You can't bring it back.*

What kinds of things could the land be used for after the mining
is completed (housing developments, parks, golf . . .)?
> *People say, "Why don't you just sell?"*
> *They've offered me seven times the amount of acreage*
> *as what I've got for my place.*
> *But then the land they offered me—*
> *my people never walked on it.*
> *It's been turned over.*
> *You can't put anything on it,*
> *can't grow anything on it.*

NOTE TO TEACHER: This lesson should not give the impression
that mining is bad and destroys the environment. We all depend
on mining each day for the everyday items we use. Rather, make sure
the students understand that we have laws to protect the environment.

The Management of Time

The pileated, with his exuberant staccato call,
his child's rendering of ocean waves
as he swoops from tree to tree,
still arrests me.

As the neighborhood falls to the chainsaw's teeth—
is hauled away and quartered—he still comes to dinner
in black and white, hammering stumps
two feet from the walk.

Is it just me that hears a blue note of surprise in his clarion cry?
Probably. My oncologist now stresses *the management of time*,
and I think of a neighbor long gone. *Well*, he said,
it made a mess of leaves.

I didn't know, then, just what to say—but I'll say it now, in case:
In this one life? Most of us don't sacrifice enough.
We take and take and take.

This World Should Be Enough

Walking the rails, looking out—
field daisies stand at attention,
and in the darkest hole along this long
hot stretch, a big trout rolls. It's the flash,
I guess, that catches my eye, and then
the daisies, until further below
a fierce-headed merganser
zagging up-current with six behind
makes me stop: *Lord, I know that this is it.*
This world should be enough. But the blue pulls
my eyes skyward, then, and I am rising
above a man with everything to lose:
he's looking downriver at a thin thread of water,
lit like a slow-burning fuse.

4.

To Have and To Hold

Flight

Our 12-seater sits on concrete
cracked and filled with rubber
on a mountaintop just a hair shorter
than the bare ridge beside, already
ripped of leaves save the tough red oak
making a stand amongst gray poplar
and the broad green flanks of pine.

This planescape begins to move, spinning
the ball of your eye into a blur that can no
longer hold the shapes of all you know, love,
and are loath to leave. The frog-green creek
is threading into its river, now, and before
that can vanish you start naming two-lanes
and hollers, holding on to cars and houses
even big mine trucks and slurry ponds,
which are tipping now, as the wings turn,
without draining.

Then the clouds. Then the letting go.
As we lift into blue the woman next to me
slackens into sleep, her elbow pressing
into the flesh of my forearm. It is soft.
She must need the sleep—at least
that is what I decide to say if questioned—
so for one hour and twenty minutes
I do not move, until the judder of down-flaps
untethers our touch, releasing us like two
balloons into our separate dreams
of things on earth. *Did I snore*, she says,
with a sheepish smile. *No*, I say, as if we
two are young lovers who still have secrets
we yearn—but cannot bear just yet—to tell.

Emergency Lane, Late June

Electric towers up the mountain
gleam—bright staples cinching

skin. Shaved smooth, cut sternum
to pelvis, I've finally sprouted again—

in thistle and milkweed; and further
down, blackberry—not ready yet,

for hands. You, whipping past on
your way to town, I know the world

seems split in half—scraped and blasted,
drowned, and set aflame. But pull over

and look up from the glass and gravel.
Do you see how the seam blooms

pink and purple? And those ugly wires
that hum? Those are honey bees

struck dumb with pollen, flying straight
to the heart of the wood.

My Son Asks How It Is Better to Have Loved and Lost

Do you remember the brushfire that burned
from the road all the way down to the creek?
Take your rod down there. Yesterday, along
the water's edge, honeybees stirred the sweet
william and on the other side, in the oak
and maple, cicadas had begun to thrum.

       Or that beagle-basset we picked up
in the median along 79? Cars whipping past
both ways and him trying one side and then
the other? No collar. Skin and bones. We turned
around and he'd just laid down. Like he knew
somebody would come along and open the door.

Pre-Carnal Knowledge

Before we do this, you should know that if you unspool
the take-up reel of my life to the moment the midwife's
scrubbed fingers slip my black-haired head back into
my mother, who closes legs as long and beautiful as mine,
smiles, and says *Yes, oh Yes,* to a man that looks
a lot like you

      until she, too, disappears blue and silent into
a woman gone skinny as a willow pedaling her bike
counter-clockwise out of the desert where the owls
she has gone looking for fold their open wings into
Saguaros hollowed by ladderback woodpeckers
long flown,

      you'll find a girl backing out of a kitchen,
having found her mother—head cradled in folded arms
on a Formica table—the side door to the garage still open,
having drawn the last man of her life into a light blue double-
winged Bel Air all the way back to boy-hood, where I can never
see who did what to make him the way men are.

Boys Will Be Boys

We were standing in the street unloading groceries,
discussing the daughter in Chicago as crows passed
overhead in the softening glow, calling out. *Why
would she do that*, I said. (Live for the summer in a

sublet no bigger than a closet without air.) *She's young,*
you said. *It's what* we *did. Right?* And the crows—
squawking whatever it is that moves them (the joy
of the flock in flight?)—seemed to confirm it. *The sky*

is built for wings, they said, heading for the spruce along
the river where they always roost. But then came fall
and with it a letter in the same cursive hand she used
in homemade cards (computer paper folded four ways):

*Not every town has boys in pickups who slow (mid-
afternoon, after school, along the main drag) to point
a deer rifle at your head and shout*, Dyke—we'll kill you
before peeling off. And get away with it, at least.

Not just because *boys will be boys* but because they
knew she knew they meant it. Separated from the flock,
how could she tell anyone, much less her parents,
who will talk, what it feels like to be alone and hunted?

In the Emergency Lane at the Bottom of the Mountain

A brown and bronze vulture plunges its head
neck deep into a hit deer's belly, whose legs
have stiffened straight as knitting needles.

He'd followed her sweet smell—uncurling
like an invisible ribbon since sun found pavement
near noon—down to the pine at the head

of the curve that rounds the blasted mountain's
torso, before flapping into the maintained grass
beside the emergency lane, where only moments

before a young mother with chestnut hair
cinched back had pulled over, yellow lights flashing,
and dragged the cooling doe a foot at a time

away from the headlamps that, come evening,
will cut through the river's late summer fog—
one eye on the car seat from which her silent

child watched; the other on the little spotted
fawn stitched into the dark hem of the wood
who will still be waiting next morning.

Reading Catalpa *near Bear Heaven Campground*

A single chickadee whirs into the rhododendron beside the boulder
I lean into just as George Ella Lyon is speaking of Virginia Woolf:
*she saw rainbows / lighting the ribs / of any animal / dead in the field
/.../ the body's / dark weight hung / against the spirit's / light.*

Then *a-dee-dee-dee* from the evergreen. Black cap. Little gray body.
Before he flits—in descending loops like a vanishing garland—
all the way to a tall spruce rising from tumbling scree, its sunlit
needles brighter for the hardwoods just swelling now with leaves.

Which turns my mind from George Ella—who as a girl in Harlan
read *Black Beauty*, then ate raw oats *to taste what is was like to be
a horse*—to Anna, who lives up the holler, and all this virtual learning
behind a screen: *In 4-5 pages, analyze a problem imbedded in a specific*

*place: how are the people, culture, and/or natural environment affected
by this problem?* How she pecked out the best answer on her phone,
wound her salt-covered Escort down the mountain through ice
and snow, and pulled into McDonald's, just to let me know.

The Kite Master

Half dune roots like dead wires hanging head high, boardwalks
dashed and flung, two-by-fours sticking willy-nilly out of sand
like bones, whale belly on my screen split and spilling plastic
on the beach, and down the way, a Trump flag tied to a pop-up
that shields an entire brood of pale flesh swathed in red and white
giving me the blues

       until my daughter's partner puts down her book, unrolls
her two-string two-grip kite, lays it flat, and then backsteps straight
into the sky. Soon she's worked it over the roiling water, and without
once getting her rainbow wings wet, begins to buzz the ocean in big
wind-popping swoops until all those heads two houses down
start turning her way in wonder.

Truth Be Told

begins the end of a thousand conversations,
but, honestly, I don't trust what comes next
as far as I can spit. If you must solemnly swear
that you've told the truth and nothing but
how tall must this tale be? I swear to God
more than I should, but only because
I'm a liar who believes in our forgiveness
whether we understand each other or not.
Hemingway said the truth's best left unsaid—
but, in the end, I always take my reader's hand.
I always say, *I do*. Because, cross my heart—
it doesn't matter what you say: It's the broken
silences.

After the Argument

After the argument, full of sorrow, and weary,
I drive until I'm standing in a river that cuts
through the second oldest mountain range
in the world. Nothing we have said has not
been said before. I catch fish after fish in this
one crooked stretch. Twenty-nine in three hours
the length of my elbow down. It's odd, this bounty
I don't deserve—of greater and greater gratitude,
and relief, with each release. When I was younger,
I'd string them up alive and straining through the gills.
Today, I cradle each one half in and out of water,
their green and gold scales—tiny mirrors that flash
a silent plea: have and hold, but only to better see,
how letting go rekindles what love used to be.

When Love Returns

I've been standing beside a mountain lake
watching clouds race across the mirror's surface
and slip beneath my feet, when love returns.
It's narrow and thin—a ribbon of breath no wider
than your tongue that splits the broom sedge,
licks a strip of sky off the water's back, lifts my eyes,
and stipples skin. Love, when it returns, is narrow and thin.
Clouds slip beneath my feet. But when I turn my back
and step towards the car, its door the mouth
of everything I can't outrun, my heart rises up
like a heavy fish. It breaks the surface of the sun.

As Through Water Bent Like Old Glass

A woman hunches over a computer screen at the kitchen table
like Narcissus before the vernal pool. Only, in this myth,
she outwits three insurance companies, pays the mortgage,
and floats a check to Utility Billing before nodding off,
before falling in and drowning, only to rise as beautiful
as the first day she met her husband, before sickness
and tears turned his head away.

  In this myth, she rises like the milkweed and green arrow
by the little pool out back, as a woman all her own, save children
who never grow old and a man who tells her, every morning,
exactly how he sees her: as through water bent like old glass,
beckoning, still offering everything he could never have.
Even if it all ends tomorrow, he says again and again—
it was enough.

Returning Me My Eyes

Down here, from my porch swing, I hear a raven
croaking somewhere overhead. And though my body
and spirit no longer align, I rise through oak
and maple, magnolia and laurel, to where
the red spruce reign. No matter why. At some
point, everyone travels only in mind, up and out,
until everything is drowned in a blue roar of sky.
And this returns me my eyes, and everything
to its place, which I see as I descend. Where
the canopy opens, white-petaled windflower blooms
thick as stars. And there, up on the bank, pink
and purple columbine fracture stones, rolling them—
over centuries—down the mountainside.

October

Willow leaves land on the pond's surface like yellow canoes.
The goldfish, having slumbered in the shadows all morning,
rise like red Kraken to swamp the little boats—but never do.

Soon, ice will ride out from the grasses and cattails, lacing blue;
the pond's eye will thicken, become glaucous and gray, but still
they'll hang, holding fast as old vows that, come spring, renew.

5.

Fifty Gardens In

Crossing the Eastern Continental Divide at Sundown

Up here, leaves of grass have all gone gold.
Ironweed and joe pye pose pink and purple riddles
to the sky, while red sumac burn like flambeaus.
But what gets me is the milkweed—
their smooth silk purses all split open
like deployment bags, billows spent,
their mission long accomplished. Somehow,
we missed the great migration and must imagine—
how 10,000 seeds pulled parachute
and crossing ridge, caught fire.

Fifty Gardens In

for Michael Stennes

Sometimes it doesn't matter how much
you water a drought-stricken plant.
It can't take what you give it. *Where the
hell were you?* its shriveled leaves say.
Look at it another way. My neighbor
Michael, would do anything for you.
Struck riding his bike visiting family
a year ago today, the doctors gave
pint after pint, but his heart—
which had given so much already—
wouldn't pump it through. Fifty gardens
in, I know this much is true: Keep an eye
on what wants to live. Give away
what you can before the season ends.

Hawks at Dusk

for William Kirk

Tonight will be the longest night
in the history of the Earth, I am told,
but even such a little eternity beggars
imagination, while the things of this world,

illuminated by the distant sun, do not.
They still deserve our attention: twelve
red-tails on the way back from your memorial
today, one on the top of a steel light post

just outside Fairfax, one crossing in flight
low over the road, and the rest in the high
arms of trees along the two-lane that splits
the George Washington and the Thomas

Jefferson National Forests. You knew this area
well. Your childhood friend said you could walk
its rocky trails in the dark, so maybe you knew
what you were doing when you took your leave of us.

They will eat carrion, hawks, but more often
are the silent shadow that precedes mercy. They
carry the wounded skyward. Will, I do not know
what wildfire raged in your heart, what wind

outflanking the hard-won line, blew up in your face,
but I'm sure you would have seen each one of them
while the rest of us, stuck in the traffic of our
crowded byways, would not. Let me tell you,

except for the one in flight, they were standing

at attention like tomb guards at the National Cemetery
who don their blue plumage in any weather,
and never forget.

This Is the Way

The morning the canyon opened,
its roaring water thundering and
its mist rising through rose light
carrying sweet white azalea into black,

the world could have been saying
It's your time to go, and I would have,
except that too few of us have ever
stepped in a river powerful enough to pin

a body to the bottom, or emerged
at day's end atop a rock cliff—
the river but a single lost thread below,
buzzards sweeping up and out

and over where you have just been:
this is the way it will be when you are
not looking, when you are pulled
backwards and up as if by a string.

Yes, the world is ending. It is ending
every day, and our feet are not even wet.

Tonight in West Virginia

Three red oak leaves, curled into a hull
with midribs for a keel, swirl downriver
on a slate blue sky veined brown by the canopy's
branches. They bounce over riffle rocks, then
fall into a hole that spits each up again,
for a time, before vanishing

        around a bend. From this side
of the Cheat, a golden lamina gilds the far bank
where green-hearted fox grapes strangle sassafras
and laurel. Just above the water: a single
monarch, the last of the passing through,
jerks upstream.

        Tonight in West Virginia, it will frost,
hard, and the few remaining leaves—scarlet, orange—
will take the same ride as all the others. Soon, I will
follow, south to my brother-in-law, newly prone
and paralyzed with a ventilator for a lullaby
in his head.

        He stood up too fast; on the way down,
hit his chin. Until now and then, all I can do is skip
stones while the sky sets the river on fire. I stoop again
and again, looking for just the right one to send
across the brilliant pool—two, three, four-five—
into the darkness on the other side.

Promise Made in Total Darkness

When we enter the Sinks—a mile-long gurgle of snow
melt and spring water that splits a high bald then slips
under a ledge of limestone—the summer blues go first,
and then spruce green, until we reach the last ripple

of light on the walls and stop. A swallow flits over,
and you, taller and bearded now, point one long
finger toward a clutch of blind beaks clamoring
above a lip of grass and clay. We wade beneath

them to the edge of the bend, step onto a boulder,
and stare into the black. You click your headlamp
forward but I swivel around to witness the quick
dipping bird flit from the flaming zero of the entrance

and into a swarm of flies. By the time I feel the ancient
wire of need keening across the space between us,
you've gone. So I click headlamp forward and step once
again into the shockingly cold water. The stream

narrows and deepens. Sand banks near the cave wall
steepen, then cake to mud. Crouched and low, I touch stone
for balance, try to catch up, but slip then slide waist deep.
How far ahead could he be? I think, and kill the light

to better hear. I call. One beat. Two. Until, "Dad?"
echoes off the opposite wall and I wait for the blade of light.
"We'll do it," you say, "but not today." No hard hats,
no extra lamps, not safe enough, yet, for the long traverse

from blue to blue beneath a field of hooves. Lights off
again, you grip my shoulder and the weight of stone
above lifts like ravens riding updraft above the ridgeline.
"Next summer," you say, gripping harder until I believe.

Calling Grackles

for Walter C. King

My last visit I was surprised he could not rise
from bed. It was Aunt Sadie, twisted like a ridge pine
by crooked knee and bent spine, who opened the door.
Leaning on a three-footed cane, she tilted her downcast
head sideways and up just enough, burst into a smile,
and shouted *Lawdy-lawd—Walter! Look who's here!*
as she turning, shuffled, waving me in.

Down the dim hallway we moved like a pair
of petals settled into a river, past the row of glass clocks
on the mantel I once begged to better see. He'd lift
one down and, careful to keep it level, place it
on the coffee table so I could watch the crystal
pendulum like a little merry-go-round
above a pond of gold, spin.

When I go you'll have these, he said, lifting a pair
of 10 x 40's the mill gifted him, a life-long engineer.
Miracles of color, song, and flight, he said, nodding to the redbird
cracking seed outside his window. I had to go—I was only
passing through on my way home for Christmas—
but not before he hacked out a paroxysm of epithets
at a plague of grackles whistling in the trees.

Come spring, he was thin skin over bone.
Black polyester suit. A few licks of black hair greased
into a part. When the six of us bent to the casket and heaved,
I was surprised how light he was. If I were given to prayer,
I'd have called on those querulous birds to lift and,
wheeling clear of the tall oak out front, flash iridescent
as the suit we lowered him in.

Beaver Pond

I walk around, casting shadows,
but your dark eye misses nothing:

a river of blackbirds seeking stubble
(in the field beyond the ridge you cannot see),
the long gray arm of maple mottled yellow
(from the dark mouth of woods to the west),
even a little green inchworm that hangs by invisible thread
stretching two toes toward your mirror—

none of this fretting by the shore,
this continual circling of dark water
good enough for the doe
who, dipping her slender neck at dusk,
nudges stars into a wobble
and for the trapped brook trout pebbled orange
who, missing his target,
shatters the moon.

Final Note

Even when I can't hear it, I hear it: the Shaver's rolling
over round wall stones and sling shot pebbles; broken ledges

fallen and drowned but full of ancient talk—the broken stems
of sea flowers, the open mouths of lamp shells filled with lime.

If the water's up, step in upstream and push slant-wise for the one
slab that still overhangs; grab the upturned edge of that bygone

ocean's bottom and tread, taking in what you can before letting go
and re-entering the now muted flow. Along the bottom, a shoal

of hognose lumber upstream; smallmouth and brook trout fin
inside a leafless tree. Before pushing up from the shallows, cleave

a school of translucent darters and hear, again, the river's swift
issuance; the rain of your lowered head streaming into sky—

down, down the rippling shallows of summer, drumming under ice.
This is no mumbled prayer against oblivion. It is the push and flutter

of a thousand seeps and springs and runs braided into a roar.
You can hear it any day—bending trees on the ridge above town,

or buffeting down Kelly Mountain, coming home. It will be
the final note—after words and understanding go—as I float

over the strange, jumbled garden, and beneath the jeweled
green tongues of fern rooted high above the shore.

The Author

BILL KING is the 2021 Heartwood Poetry Award winner and author of the chapbook *The Letting Go*. A professor of English at Davis & Elkins College in Elkins, West Virginia, his work appears in *100 Word Story*, *The Cincinnati Review*, *Appalachian Review*, and other journals. This full-length collection, his first, commemorates a life lived in the Blue Ridge and Appalachian Mountains.